Reflection Therapy

Dr. Sharon Giammatteo
Dr. Thomas Giammatteo

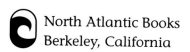

North Atlantic Books
Berkeley, California

Important note: Medical knowledge is ever-changing. As new research and clinical experience broaden our knowledge, changes in treatment and drug therapy may be required. The authors and editors of the material herein have consulted sources believed to be reliable in their efforts to provide information that is complete and in accord with the standards accepted at the time of publication. However, in view of the possibility of human error, neither the authors, editors, or publisher, nor any other party who has been involved in the preparation of this work, warrants that the information contained herein is in every respect accurate or complete, and they are not responsible for any errors or omissions or for the results obtained from use of such information. Readers are encouraged to confirm the information contained herein with other sources. For example, readers are advised to check each technique to be certain that the information contained in this publication is accurate and that changes have not been made in the recommended practice or in possible contraindications of it. This recommendation is of particular importance in connection with new therapies.

Some of the names and processes referred to in this book are in fact registered trademarks or proprietary names even though specific reference to this fact is not always made in the text. Therefore, the appearance of a name without designation as proprietary is not to be construed as a representation by the publisher that it is in the public domain.

Published by North Atlantic Books
P.O. Box 12327
Berkeley, California 94712

Printed in Singapore
Cover and book design by Catherine E. Campaigne

North Atlantic Books' publications are available through most bookstores. For further information, call 800-337-2665 or visit our website at www.northatlanticbooks.com.

Substantial discounts on bulk quantities are available to corporations, professional associations, and other organizations. For details and discount information, contact our special sales department.

Reflection Therapy is sponsored by the Society for the Study of Native Arts and Sciences, a nonprofit educational corporation whose goals are to develop an educational and crosscultural perspective linking various scientific, social, and artistic fields; to nurture a holistic view of arts, sciences, humanities, and healing; and to publish and distribute literature on the relationship of mind, body, and nature.

1 2 3 4 5 6 7 8 9 / 06 05 04 03 02 01

Table of Contents

What is Reflection Therapy?

*R*eflection Therapy is a neuro-cognitive approach to medicine and an introduction to a new domain of mind-body science. It addresses experimentally a mostly unprobed area of healing—and of human consciousness in general—in which visualizations of images (color, radiance, shape, etc.) can lead to psychosomatic changes via some as-yet-unknown form of cellular or trans-cellular communication.

Reflection Therapy is a totally original invention of Sharon and Tom Giammatteo; however, it is not the only medical practice based on transformation of visual images and subliminal instructions into mind-body processes. It is possible that homeopathic medicine operates in a similar fashion by transducing molecular form initially through nanopharmacology, succussion, and potentization, and subsequently through systemic resonance from the remedy's initial triggered effects. Visualization by itself is the currency of a number of healing systems in diverse cultures (for instance, *tangkas* in Tibet, sand-paintings and chant symbols among the Navaho of the American Southwest, hare and peacock icons in Laos, and even tarot-like mandalas in early Western medicine). Perhaps "magical" cave-paintings viewed by firelight during the late Stone Age were innocent forerunners of the first "reflection therapy."

The history of development of Reflection Therapy is a separate story. Two persons, Sharon Weiselfish (now Giammatteo) and Thomas Giammatteo, each on their own individual journeys of growth and development, brought very different areas of expertise together to develop a simple but remarkably effective approach that combined communication in computer technology with neurologic science. Both Reflection Therapy founders are Master Clinical Hypnotherapists trained in multiple body/mind therapies as well as various approaches of psychotherapeutics. They are firm believers in self-healing.

During the 1980s when Weiselfish was studying for her doctoral degree in manual and cranial therapies for the neurologic client, she carried out research in the clinical neurosciences, in particular the field of photic stimulation. Guided by this formative research and years of subsequent study in the neurosciences, she applied her sophisticated diagnostic skills to the development of a new modality from the assessment of biologic rhythms. As specific regional and neurologic sites were palpated, she gradually developed maps and trajectories of emotional, cognitive, and anatomical states.

Throughout his studies in computer technology, Giammatteo meanwhile attained skills in language, graphics, color, and shape. Using Quark, a graphic design software program prevalent in book publishing, he cultivated an ability to project computerized images in cognitively and subliminally dynamic shapes, colors, and shades.

Their joint process of final confirmation for the exercises in this book was both empirical and experiential. As Sharon performed Cranial Therapy and other body/mind modalities on Tom, she induced in him a delta trance-like clinical hypnotherapeutic state and then read to him affirmations. In a delta state his affirmations elicited biologic rhythms aligned with particular locations. Tom then chose the shape, size, color, and shade of the graphics for each affirmation.

Blending separate modalities and technologies has culminated in the birth of Reflection Therapy. Color therapy is a normal tool of art therapy. Photic stimulation is a recognized modality for stimulating the brain through color. Sharon and Tom Giammatteo have essentially combined art therapy and color therapy with photic stimulation. The skills and knowledge of this hybridized area of healing were then integrated with different techniques of body/mind therapy and clinical hypnotherapy, and finally melded into the art of computer graphics.

Sharon's research into simple new self-healing modalities also includes a direct manual-therapy approach she has named Neurofascial Process.* This hands-on series of exercises and techniques can be used to transform pain, disability, disease, and emotional stress. Reflection Therapy, in fact, unites its own neuro-cognitive method with the manual aspects of Neurofascial Process.

---

*For an historical perspective on Neurofascial Process, see *Body Wisdom, Simple Techniques for Optimal Health* by Sharon (Weiselfish) Giammatteo (North Atlantic Books, 2002). The hands-on procedures are easy for anyone to learn and practice, as pictures and photographs bring clarity to words. *Reflection Therapy* is, in a sense, a compendium for *Body Wisdom*. Use the exercises and different approaches in both books for synergistic effect.

How to Perform Reflection Therapy

*T*he following exercises were contributed by Sharon W. Giammatteo, Ph.D., P.T. and Thomas Giammatteo, D.C., P.T. As self-healing modes, they do not replace therapy with a counselor or psychotherapist, but they can be used by all practitioners, all disciplines, all clients (in conjunction with other therapies or by themselves). The exercises in this book enhance facets of relaxation and the degree and depth of recovery from a number of ailments. There are (thus far) no significant precautions or contraindications.

The exercises are deliberately thirty seconds duration each (the amount of time you spend looking at the picture). That makes them 'homeopathic doses.' Potentized remedies of this sort operate especially powerfully on mental and other subtle levels.

The client can do one exercise a day, or several exercises a day. He or she can perform these exercises more frequently, or less frequently, for example one exercise a week. He can focus on any one exercise, or as many exercises as desired, during any time frame. The exercises can be practiced together, or separately during the day. They can be practiced for a week, for a month, or for a year, etc.

No specific exercise should be practiced more than one time (thirty seconds) per day. If an exercise is practiced more than one time per day or longer than thirty seconds per day, an 'overuse syndrome' ensues; the curative effect is paradoxically under-emphasized and reduced.

The reader should follow the instructions listed under each exercise. If the exercise begins with: "Close your eyes." and does not state: "Sit down." or "Stand up," then it is best to perform the exercise occasionally in sitting, occasionally in standing positions.

Do not let trying to imagine how these exercises work get in your way. They are not "normal" exercises in the usual sense of kinetics, duration, or linear cause and effect. They are more like the quantum events by which matter is turned into energy (and vice versa) in the chloroplasts of plants, or the process whereby a blastula becomes a full organism through the specific potentiation of its cells.

Directions
How to perform Reflection Therapy with Photic Stimulation
(Looking at an image to influence mind)

1. Choose the exercise.

2. Prepare "equipment" that may be required (for some exercises).

3. Look at the colored image, opposite the written exercise, for ten seconds.

4. Perform the exercise.

5. Look at the image again for 30 seconds.

Reflection Therapy

Free Writing for Development of Expression

1. Close your eyes.

2. Put a thought in your mind: "I am inside my body."

3. Repeat this thought ten repetitions.

4. Write. Use a blank piece of lined paper. Use a pen.

Creation of Space

1. Use multiple colors of crayons, rather then pen or magic markers.

2. Use a blank page, without lines or borders.

3. Close your eyes.

4. Put a thought in your mind: "There are many avenues of expression."

5. Repeat this thought ten repetitions.

6. Draw.

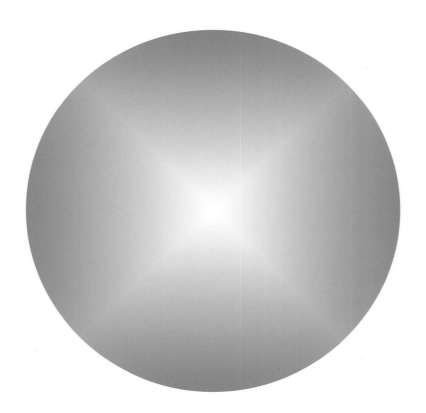

Lowering Threshold of Stress for Re-education of Stress Management

1. Lower the TV until you can barely hear the words on the TV.

2. Turn up the music on the stereo to moderate volume, not blaring, so that you can no longer hear the words on the TV.

3. Focus your eyes on the TV. "Listen" in your mind to the words of the stereo music.

4. Perform this exercise for 3 minutes.

5. Shut off the music.

6. Listen to the words on the TV.

7. Breathe. Focus attention on: inhalation and exhalation.

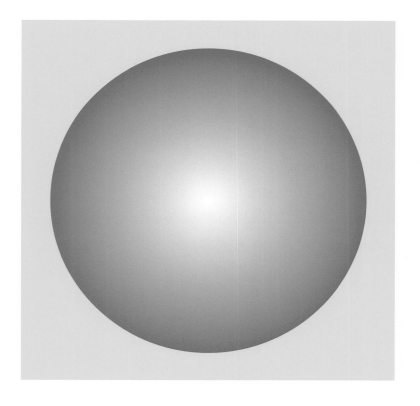

Letting Go of
Reaction Response

1. Look at your eyes in the mirror. Focus on your eyes for 30 seconds.

2. Close your eyes.

3. Put a thought in your mind: "I am able to see."

4. Repeat this thought ten repetitions.

5. Attempt to look into your eyes with your eyes closed.

6. Continue for 30 seconds.

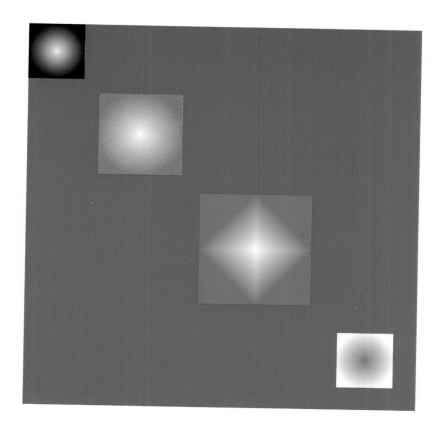

Looking at Behavior That Induces Stress

1. Be seated in a quiet place.

2. Close your eyes.

3. Think of the day before (yesterday, not today). Put a thought in your mind: "I am visiting yesterday."

4. Repeat this thought ten repetitions.

5. What behavior first comes to mind?

6. Do not judge the behavior, just reflect upon the behavior. Reflect upon the behavior for 30 seconds.

Letting Go of Stress-Inducing Thoughts

1. Be seated in a quiet place.

2. Close your eyes.

3. Ask yourself: "Am I thinking?"

4. Repeat this thought ten repetitions.

5. Allow yourself to consider any new thought which comes into your mind.

6. Focus on this thought for 30 seconds.

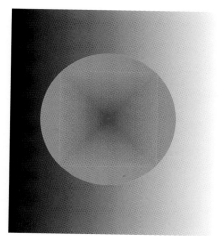

Performance-Based Anxiety Release

1. Stand up.
2. Close your eyes.
3. Put a thought in your mind: "I am going to work."
4. Repeat this thought ten repetitions.
5. Do not move; remain standing.
6. Keep your eyes closed, while standing, during 30 seconds after you finish repeating the thought 10 times.

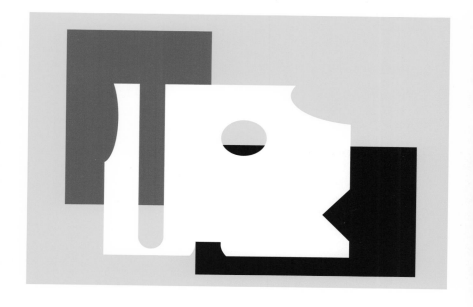

Relaxation-Based Anxiety Release

1. Lie down surrounded by 5 soft pillows.

2. Close your eyes.

3. Put a thought in your mind: "I am going to relax."

4. Repeat this thought ten repetitions.

5. Do not move; remain lying down, snuggled among pillows. (Pillows cannot be substituted by blankets or other supportive equipment.)

6. Keep your eyes closed for 30 seconds after you finish repeating the thought 10 times.

Phobia Release

1. Let your mind wander. Do not be focused on any particular thought.

2. Walk randomly around the room. The room cannot be cluttered.

3. After 30 seconds: close your eyes and stop walking.

4. Immediately put the thought in your mind: "I am not afraid."

5. Repeat the thought ten repetitions.

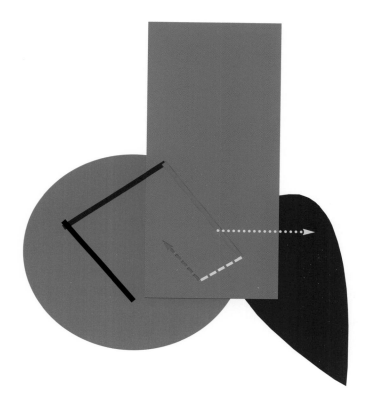

Incorporation of Obsession Disassociation

1. Close your eyes.

2. Make your hands into tight fists.

3. Put a thought into your mind: "I am opening my hands."

4. Do not open your hands. Keep them fisted tightly.

5. Repeat the thought ten repetitions.

6. Then open your hands. Keep your eyes closed.

7. Put a second thought in your mind: "I can open my hands. I am looking at my open hands."

8. Repeat the thought ten repetitions.

9. Keep your eyes closed for 30 seconds.

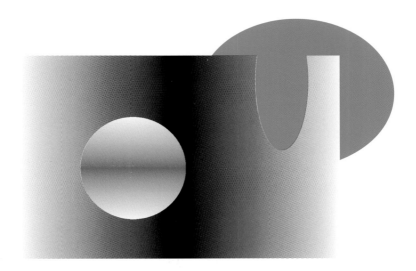

Alleviation of Mood

1. Close your eyes.

2. Smile.

3. Smile wider.

4. Smile until you feel a stretch on your lips.

5. Put a thought in your mind: "I know how to smile."

6. Repeat the thought ten repetitions.

7. Maintain the wide smile while you repeat the thought.

8. Maintain the smile for 30 seconds.

Elevation of Mood

1. Close your eyes.

2. Put both hands gently on the sides of your face.

3. Rub your hands gently on the sides of your face.

4. Put a thought in your mind: "My touch is soft."

5. Repeat the thought ten repetitions.

6. Keep rubbing your face gently for 30 seconds.

Attachment Generation

1. Close your eyes.

2. Put a thought in your mind: "I am not alone."

3. Repeat the thought ten repetitions.

4. Hold a soft pillow between your arms. Hug the pillow. All of your strength is used to hug the pillow.

5. Put a thought in your mind: "This feels like I am not alone."

6. Repeat the thought ten repetitions.

7. Continue to hug the pillow tight against your body for 30 seconds.

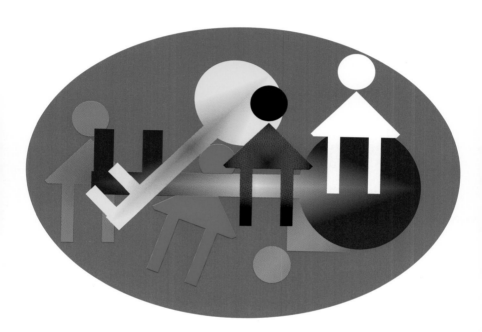

Lowering the Reaction to Claustrophobia

1. Stand next to the closet door.

2. Open the door. Hold onto the door knob.

3. Close your eyes.

4. Put a thought in your mind: "I am inside the closet. I am not afraid."

5. Repeat the thought ten repetitions.

6. Close the door. Stand holding the door knob for 30 seconds. Do not enter the closet.

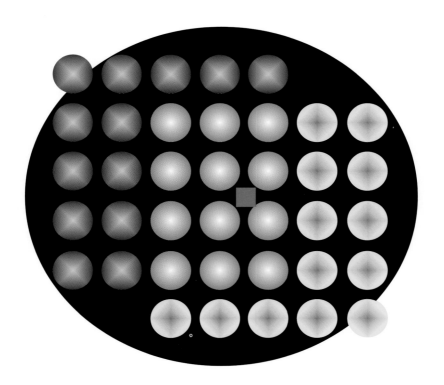

Lowering the Response to Nightmares

1. Sit down at a table. Have a black magic marker available, and a blank piece of black paper.

2. Close your eyes. Hold the black magic marker in your hand, touching the piece of black paper.

3. Put a thought in your mind: "My nightmare is white."

4. Repeat the thought ten repetitions.

5. Image that the paper is white, and your magic marker is green, with your eyes closed. Continue to image a piece of white paper with green drawings on the white paper for 30 seconds.

6. Be sure to open your eyes after 30 seconds of reflection on the white paper and green drawing.

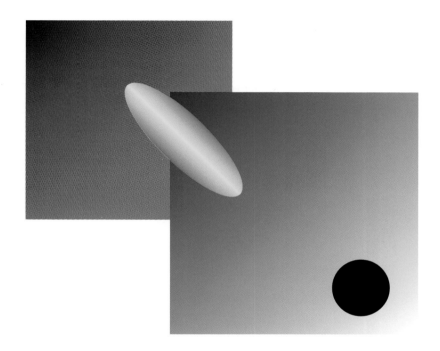

Lessen the Reaction to Hallucinations

1. Close your eyes. Stand up. Sit down. Continue to stand up and then sit down ten repetitions.

2. Then sit down.

3. Put a thought in your mind: "I am dreaming."

4. Repeat the thought ten repetitions.

5. Then stand up.

6. Put a thought in your mind: "I am dreaming."

7. Then sit down.

8. With your eyes remaining shut, do not focus on any thought.

9. Continue for 30 seconds to reflect on no thought.

10. Be sure to open your eyes after 30 seconds.

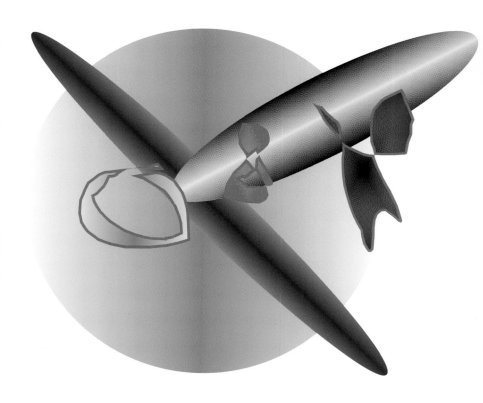

Lessen the Limbic Response to People

1. Close your eyes.

2. Put a thought in your mind: "I am not responsible for my reaction to_____." (You must use a person's name.)

3. Repeat the thought ten repetitions.

4. Open your eyes after 30 seconds.

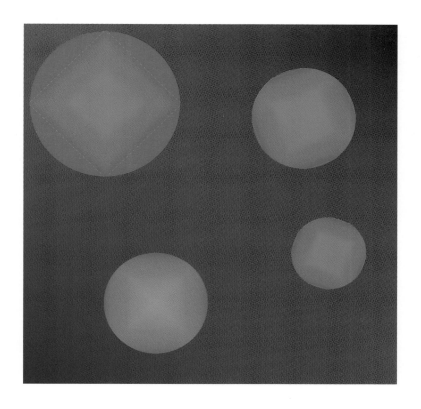

Lessen the Limbic Response to Situations

1. Close your eyes.

2. Put a thought in your mind: "I am not responsible for my reaction to. . . ." (You must mention the situation, for example: "I am not responsible for my reaction to working." "I am not responsible for my reaction to waking up in the middle of the night." "I am not responsible for my reaction to scary movies." "I am not responsible for my reaction to lesbian and gay persons." "I am not responsible for my reaction to Jewish, Black, Indian people," and more.

   NOTE: This non-responsibility to a reaction definitely does not mean a person is not responsible for his / her actions. It is necessary to remove the guilt of association and thought responses before a person can reflect upon behaviors which are discriminatory.

3. Repeat the thought ten repetitions.

4. Open your eyes after 30 seconds.

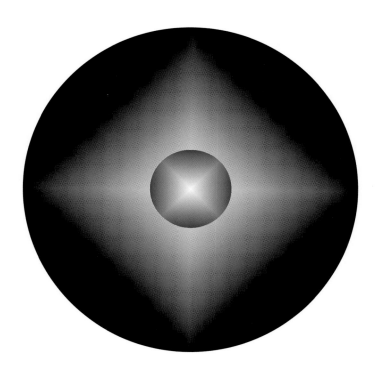

Lowering Paranoid Responsiveness

1. Stand up against the wall. Stand close to the wall. Face the wall.

2. Close your eyes.

3. Put a thought in your mind: "Pressure does not frighten me."

4. Repeat the thought ten repetitions.

5. Stay up against the wall, facing the wall, for 30 seconds.

Appreciation for Food

1. Stand next to the refrigerator.

2. Hold onto the handle of the refrigerator.

3. Close your eyes.

4. Put a thought in your mind: "I see inside the refrigerator."

5. Repeat the thought ten repetitions.

6. Open the refrigerator door slightly.

7. Keep your eyes closed.

8. Put a thought in your mind: "I see inside the refrigerator."

9. Repeat the thought ten repetitions.

10. Close the refrigerator door. Open your eyes after the door is closed.

Letting Go of Fear

1. Place one hand on your heart.

2. Close your eyes.

3. Reach out with the other arm straight ahead.

4. Make a fist with the hand of the arm which is reaching out.

5. Put a thought in your mind: "I am afraid of nothing."

6. Repeat the thought ten repetitions.

7. Now, reach out with the same arm above your head.

8. Open and close your fist ten repetitions.

9. Then keep your hand in a fist.

10. Put a thought in your mind: "I am afraid of no one."

11. Lower both arms and open your hands. Open your eyes.

Learning to Be Alone

1. Perform the exercise with a chair behind you.

2. Stand in front of the chair.

3. Close your eyes.

4. Sit down on the chair with your eyes closed.

5. Perform stand-to-sit and sit-to-stand ten repetitions. Keep your eyes closed.

6. Sit down with your eyes still closed.

7. Put a thought in your mind: "Is being alone enough for me. Not tomorrow. Yes for today."

8. Repeat the thought ten repetitions.

9. Open your eyes.

Attitude Adjustment

1. Sit on a chair.

2. Look at your surroundings for ten seconds.

3. Close your eyes.

4. Put a thought in your mind: "I love my surroundings. I am at peace with my surroundings."

5. Repeat the thought ten repetitions.

6. Open your eyes.

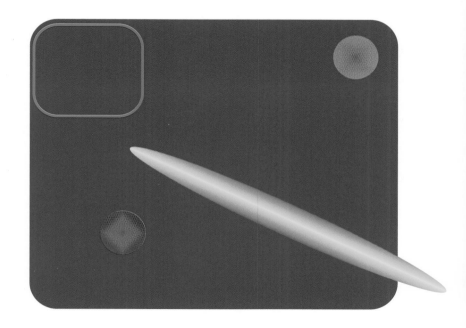

Alleviation of Pain

1. Stand.

2. Place both hands over your heart.

3. Close your eyes.

4. Put a thought in your mind: "Judge me not. I am me."

5. Repeat the thought ten repetitions.

6. Open your eyes.

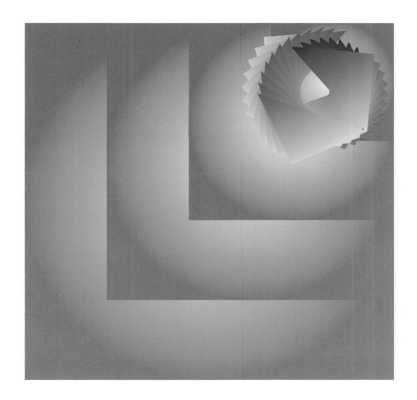

Talking

1. Stand with your back up against the wall.

2. Close your eyes.

3. Turn around. Press your nose very lightly against the wall. Keep your nose pressed lightly against the wall for ten seconds.

4. Put a thought in your mind: "I want to speak out. Please allow me to speak out."

5. Repeat the thought ten repetitions.

6. Turn around. Your back is now against the wall.

7. Put a thought in your mind: "I am speaking out."

8. Repeat the thought ten repetitions.

9. Open your eyes.

Generating Hope

1. Sit or stand.

2. Close your eyes.

3. Put a thought in your mind: "Hope means letting go of me. I am letting go of me. Now I can feel me."

4. Repeat the thought ten repetitions.

5. Open your eyes.

Temper Reduction

1. Sit. Open your eyes as wide as possible. Keep you eyes very **wide** open for ten seconds.

2. Close your eyes.

3. Put a thought in your mind: "I feel better now. My eyes are helping me relax."

4. Repeat the thought ten repetitions.

5. Open your eyes.

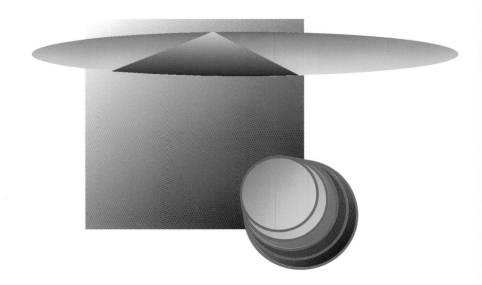

Feeling Safe

1. Close your eyes.

2. Ask yourself: "Do I want to sit down or stand up?" Answer your question.

3. Open your eyes. Sit down or stand up according to your answer.

4. Close your eyes.

5. Put a thought in your mind: "I can do whatever I want whenever I want to do it."

6. Repeat the thought ten repetitions.

7. Open your eyes.

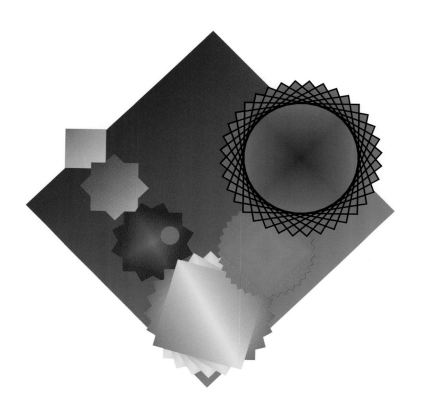

Laughing

1. Smile. Say out loud: "Ha."

2. Close your eyes.

3. Say out loud: "Ha." Smile. Say out loud: "Ha."

4. Put a thought in your mind: "I can smile." And say out loud "Ha" all at the same time.

5. Repeat the thought ten repetitions.

6. Smile and say out loud: "Ha"

7. Open your eyes.

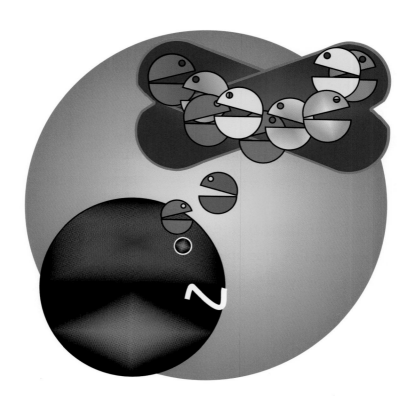

Feeling Joy

1. Purse your lips. Squeeze your upper and lower lips together.

2. Close your eyes. Keep your lips pursed.

3. Put a thought in your mind: "I love my lips. What do my lips feel like when they are not pursed?"

4. Repeat the thought ten repetitions, while your lips are pursed.

5. Open your lips wide and wider.

6. Keep your lips wide open for ten seconds.

7. Open your eyes.

Calming Down

1. Sit. Slouch. Be relaxed.

2. Close your eyes.

3. Put a thought in your mind: "I think relax. I like relax. I want relax. I know relax."

4. Repeat the thought ten repetitions.

5. Open your eyes.

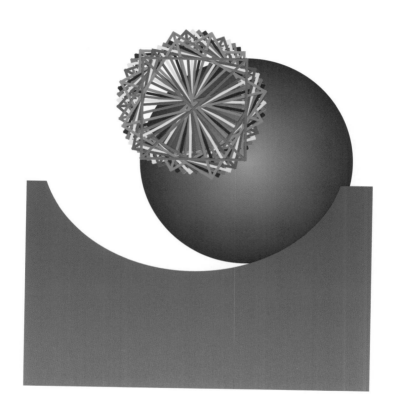

Having Movement

1. Stand.

2. Close your eyes.

3. Move your toes. Really move your toes. Move your toes more. Move your toes for one minute.

4. Put a thought in your mind: "My toes move. My toes move a lot. My toes could move a lot more."

5. Open your eyes.

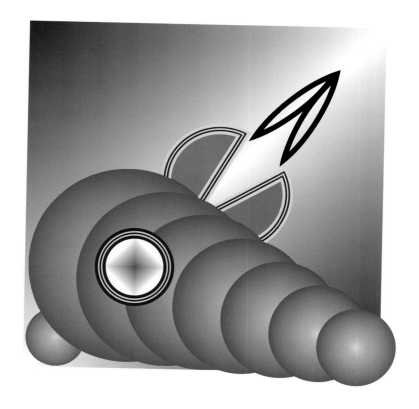

Lowering Threshold of Stress

1. Close your eyes.

2. Think about stress. Think for one minute about stress. Then think for 30 seconds about your stress.

3. Put a thought in your mind: "I do not like stress. I want no stress."

4. Repeat the thought ten repetitions.

5. Open your eyes.

Eyes Calming

1. Close your eyes.

2. Place the pads of your fingers lightly over your eyes.

3. Put a thought in your mind: "My fingers do not feel heavy on my eyes."

4. Repeat the thought ten repetitions.

5. Open your eyes.

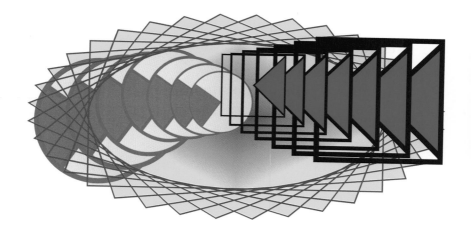

Breathing Deeply

1. Close your eyes.

2. Look at your eyelids with your eyes closed.

3. Put a thought in your mind: "I can breathe while I look at my eyelids."

4. Repeat the thought ten repetitions.

5. Open your eyes.

Recommendation Sheet

Perform the following Exercises

- ☐ Exercise # 1
- ☐ Exercise # 2
- ☐ Exercise # 3
- ☐ Exercise # 4
- ☐ Exercise # 5
- ☐ Exercise # 6
- ☐ Exercise # 7
- ☐ Exercise # 8
- ☐ Exercise # 9
- ☐ Exercise # 10
- ☐ Exercise # 11
- ☐ Exercise # 12
- ☐ Exercise # 13
- ☐ Exercise # 14
- ☐ Exercise # 15
- ☐ Exercise # 16
- ☐ Exercise # 17
- ☐ Exercise # 18
- ☐ Exercise # 19
- ☐ Exercise # 20
- ☐ Exercise # 21
- ☐ Exercise # 22
- ☐ Exercise # 23
- ☐ Exercise # 24
- ☐ Exercise # 25
- ☐ Exercise # 26
- ☐ Exercise # 27
- ☐ Exercise # 28
- ☐ Exercise # 29
- ☐ Exercise # 30
- ☐ Exercise # 31
- ☐ Exercise # 32
- ☐ Exercise # 33
- ☐ Exercise # 34
- ☐ Exercise # 35

- ☐ Exercise # 1
- ☐ Exercise # 2
- ☐ Exercise # 3
- ☐ Exercise # 4
- ☐ Exercise # 5
- ☐ Exercise # 6
- ☐ Exercise # 7
- ☐ Exercise # 8
- ☐ Exercise # 9
- ☐ Exercise # 10
- ☐ Exercise # 11
- ☐ Exercise # 12
- ☐ Exercise # 13
- ☐ Exercise # 14
- ☐ Exercise # 15
- ☐ Exercise # 16
- ☐ Exercise # 17
- ☐ Exercise # 18
- ☐ Exercise # 19
- ☐ Exercise # 20
- ☐ Exercise # 21
- ☐ Exercise # 22
- ☐ Exercise # 23
- ☐ Exercise # 24
- ☐ Exercise # 25
- ☐ Exercise # 26
- ☐ Exercise # 27
- ☐ Exercise # 28
- ☐ Exercise # 29
- ☐ Exercise # 30
- ☐ Exercise # 31
- ☐ Exercise # 32
- ☐ Exercise # 33
- ☐ Exercise # 34
- ☐ Exercise # 35

Recommendation Sheet

Perform the following Exercises

☐ Exercise # 1	☐ Exercise # 13	☐ Exercise # 25
☐ Exercise # 2	☐ Exercise # 14	☐ Exercise # 26
☐ Exercise # 3	☐ Exercise # 15	☐ Exercise # 27
☐ Exercise # 4	☐ Exercise # 16	☐ Exercise # 28
☐ Exercise # 5	☐ Exercise # 17	☐ Exercise # 29
☐ Exercise # 6	☐ Exercise # 18	☐ Exercise # 30
☐ Exercise # 7	☐ Exercise # 19	☐ Exercise # 31
☐ Exercise # 8	☐ Exercise # 20	☐ Exercise # 32
☐ Exercise # 9	☐ Exercise # 21	☐ Exercise # 33
☐ Exercise # 10	☐ Exercise # 22	☐ Exercise # 34
☐ Exercise # 11	☐ Exercise # 23	☐ Exercise # 35
☐ Exercise # 12	☐ Exercise # 24	

☐ Exercise # 1	☐ Exercise # 13	☐ Exercise # 25
☐ Exercise # 2	☐ Exercise # 14	☐ Exercise # 26
☐ Exercise # 3	☐ Exercise # 15	☐ Exercise # 27
☐ Exercise # 4	☐ Exercise # 16	☐ Exercise # 28
☐ Exercise # 5	☐ Exercise # 17	☐ Exercise # 29
☐ Exercise # 6	☐ Exercise # 18	☐ Exercise # 30
☐ Exercise # 7	☐ Exercise # 19	☐ Exercise # 31
☐ Exercise # 8	☐ Exercise # 20	☐ Exercise # 32
☐ Exercise # 9	☐ Exercise # 21	☐ Exercise # 33
☐ Exercise # 10	☐ Exercise # 22	☐ Exercise # 34
☐ Exercise # 11	☐ Exercise # 23	☐ Exercise # 35
☐ Exercise # 12	☐ Exercise # 24	

Recommendation Sheet

Perform the following Exercises

☐ Exercise # 1	☐ Exercise # 13	☐ Exercise # 25
☐ Exercise # 2	☐ Exercise # 14	☐ Exercise # 26
☐ Exercise # 3	☐ Exercise # 15	☐ Exercise # 27
☐ Exercise # 4	☐ Exercise # 16	☐ Exercise # 28
☐ Exercise # 5	☐ Exercise # 17	☐ Exercise # 29
☐ Exercise # 6	☐ Exercise # 18	☐ Exercise # 30
☐ Exercise # 7	☐ Exercise # 19	☐ Exercise # 31
☐ Exercise # 8	☐ Exercise # 20	☐ Exercise # 32
☐ Exercise # 9	☐ Exercise # 21	☐ Exercise # 33
☐ Exercise # 10	☐ Exercise # 22	☐ Exercise # 34
☐ Exercise # 11	☐ Exercise # 23	☐ Exercise # 35
☐ Exercise # 12	☐ Exercise # 24	

☐ Exercise # 1	☐ Exercise # 13	☐ Exercise # 25
☐ Exercise # 2	☐ Exercise # 14	☐ Exercise # 26
☐ Exercise # 3	☐ Exercise # 15	☐ Exercise # 27
☐ Exercise # 4	☐ Exercise # 16	☐ Exercise # 28
☐ Exercise # 5	☐ Exercise # 17	☐ Exercise # 29
☐ Exercise # 6	☐ Exercise # 18	☐ Exercise # 30
☐ Exercise # 7	☐ Exercise # 19	☐ Exercise # 31
☐ Exercise # 8	☐ Exercise # 20	☐ Exercise # 32
☐ Exercise # 9	☐ Exercise # 21	☐ Exercise # 33
☐ Exercise # 10	☐ Exercise # 22	☐ Exercise # 34
☐ Exercise # 11	☐ Exercise # 23	☐ Exercise # 35
☐ Exercise # 12	☐ Exercise # 24	

Recommendation Sheet

Perform the following Exercises

- ☐ Exercise # 1
- ☐ Exercise # 2
- ☐ Exercise # 3
- ☐ Exercise # 4
- ☐ Exercise # 5
- ☐ Exercise # 6
- ☐ Exercise # 7
- ☐ Exercise # 8
- ☐ Exercise # 9
- ☐ Exercise # 10
- ☐ Exercise # 11
- ☐ Exercise # 12
- ☐ Exercise # 13
- ☐ Exercise # 14
- ☐ Exercise # 15
- ☐ Exercise # 16
- ☐ Exercise # 17
- ☐ Exercise # 18
- ☐ Exercise # 19
- ☐ Exercise # 20
- ☐ Exercise # 21
- ☐ Exercise # 22
- ☐ Exercise # 23
- ☐ Exercise # 24
- ☐ Exercise # 25
- ☐ Exercise # 26
- ☐ Exercise # 27
- ☐ Exercise # 28
- ☐ Exercise # 29
- ☐ Exercise # 30
- ☐ Exercise # 31
- ☐ Exercise # 32
- ☐ Exercise # 33
- ☐ Exercise # 34
- ☐ Exercise # 35

- ☐ Exercise # 1
- ☐ Exercise # 2
- ☐ Exercise # 3
- ☐ Exercise # 4
- ☐ Exercise # 5
- ☐ Exercise # 6
- ☐ Exercise # 7
- ☐ Exercise # 8
- ☐ Exercise # 9
- ☐ Exercise # 10
- ☐ Exercise # 11
- ☐ Exercise # 12
- ☐ Exercise # 13
- ☐ Exercise # 14
- ☐ Exercise # 15
- ☐ Exercise # 16
- ☐ Exercise # 17
- ☐ Exercise # 18
- ☐ Exercise # 19
- ☐ Exercise # 20
- ☐ Exercise # 21
- ☐ Exercise # 22
- ☐ Exercise # 23
- ☐ Exercise # 24
- ☐ Exercise # 25
- ☐ Exercise # 26
- ☐ Exercise # 27
- ☐ Exercise # 28
- ☐ Exercise # 29
- ☐ Exercise # 30
- ☐ Exercise # 31
- ☐ Exercise # 32
- ☐ Exercise # 33
- ☐ Exercise # 34
- ☐ Exercise # 35